GW00360154

Paris Scenes

Ian Brinton is a graduate from Gonville and Caius College, Cambridge, who has spent nearly forty years as a Secondary School teacher in five different schools around the country. Since retirement in 2009 he has become a full-time writer of both poetry and criticism. For some years he edited the magazine *The Use of English* for The English Association and is now co-editor of both *Tears in the Fence* and *SNOW*. He has been closely involved with the setting up of the Cambridge University Modern Poetry Archive and reviews regularly for both *The London Magazine* and *Golden Handcuffs Review*.

Sally Castle has designed covers and illustrated over thirty books for Two Rivers Press. She has a reputation for original hand lettering, and a particular interest in linocut printmaking, environmental lettering and mixed media artwork. Notable public work includes the Walking Words panels at Chatham Place in Reading and the Forbury Square stone, also in Reading. As well as commissioned work, her experimental lettering and paintings are regularly exhibited in galleries and exhibitions.

Poetry in translation by Two Rivers Press

René Noyau, *Earth on fire and other poems* translated by Gérard Noyau (2021)
Maria Teresa Horta, *Point of Honour* translated by Lesley Saunders (2019)
Henri Michaux, *Storms under the Skin* translated by Jane Draycott (2017)
John Pilling & Peter Robinson (eds.), *The Rilke of Ruth Speirs:*
   New Poems, Duino Elegies, Sonnets to Orpheus & Others (2015)
Arthur Rimbaud, *The Drunken Boat* translated by Geoff Sawers (1999)

Also by Two Rivers Poets

William Bedford, *The Dancers of Colbek* (2020)
Kate Behrens, *Man with Bombe Alaska* (2016)
Kate Behrens, *Penumbra* (2019)
Conor Carville, *English Martyrs* (2019)
Claire Dyer, *Interference Effects* (2016)
Claire Dyer, *Yield* (2020)
John Froy, *Sandpaper & Seahorses* (2018)
James Harpur, *The Examined Life* (2021)
Ian House, *Just a Moment* (2020)
Rosie Jackson & Graham Burchell, *Two Girls and a Beehive* (2020)
Gill Learner, *Chill Factor* (2016)
Sue Leigh, *Chosen Hill* (2018)
Becci Louise, *Octopus Medicine* (2017)
Mairi MacInnes, *Amazing Memories of Childhood, etc.* (2016)
Steven Matthews, *On Magnetism* (2017)
James Peake, *Reaction Time of Glass* (2019)
Peter Robinson & David Inshaw, *Bonjour Mr Inshaw* (2020)
Lesley Saunders, *Nominy-Dominy* (2018)
Jack Thacker, *Handling* (2018)
Susan Utting, *Half the Human Race* (2017)
Jean Watkins, *Precarious Lives* (2018)

Paris Scenes

Tableaux Parisiens

by Charles Baudelaire

Translated by Ian Brinton
Illustrated by Sally Castle

TWO RIVERS PRESS

First published in the UK in 2021 by Two Rivers Press
7 Denmark Road, Reading RG1 5PA
www.tworiverspress.com

ISBN 978-1-909747-86-9

1 2 3 4 5 6 7 8 9

Two Rivers Press is represented in the UK by Inpress Ltd
and distributed by Ingram Publisher Services UK.

Cover design by Nadja Guggi with an illustration by Sally Castle
Text design by Nadja Guggi and typeset in Parisine and Celeste

Printed and bound in Great Britain by Biddles, King's Lynn

Acknowledgements

One of these translations has previously appeared in *Litter* magazine.

Contents

Tableaux Parisiens

This section of *Les Fleurs du Mal* contains eighteen poems which record a twenty-four-hour tour of the city: a type of Joycean journey from the point of view of a Parisian Odysseus. As Martin Turnell suggested in his 1972 study of Baudelaire, this sequence of poems moves beyond being incidental glimpses of the city and becomes 'an attempt by the poet to re-establish contact with the world of common experience, to escape from the self'.

The sequence opens with 'Paysage' and it offers the reader a lofty view as it might have appeared to a Quasimodo gazing down on the city, 'Les deux mains au menton', who gives us a picture of what we might expect to see in the ensuing seventeen poems: the poet gazing at 'les grands ciels' prompting him to contemplate visions of eternity. His plan to 'observe the passing of the seasons', brings to mind an almost eighteenth-century gaze of measured distance visualising gardens with their 'jets d'eau'. The suggestion of an Eden in which birds are 'chantant soir et matin' reveals, however, a mistaken assumption about eternity and the poet's yearning desire for an uninterrupted vision in which the turmoil of the street knocks in vain at his window is rudely shattered by the second poem in the sequence, 'Le Soleil' ('The Eye of Day'). In the mercilessly hot post-lapsarian world the sun is recognised as father to both worm as well as rose: poverty, disease and death will haunt this landscape of the city.

The poet's movement from the lofty visions of his attic pleasure-dome down to the darkest corners of the second poem echoes the opening of Edgar Allan Poe's 1840 tale *The Man of the Crowd*, a story which Baudelaire had referred to in his article 'The Painter of Modern Life', in which he looked at the drawings of Constantin Guys. In his article Baudelaire focuses on Poe's narrator, who sits in a café looking through the shop window to enjoy 'the sight of the passing crowd' and in doing so identifies himself with all the thoughts that are moving around him. As the man's curiosity is aroused by what he sees so his vision shifts from what Poe had termed a 'generalizing turn' to a descent into detail. The figure in Poe's story is drawn increasingly away from his happy mood into a contemplation of those individual aspects of the crowd in which he discovers darker and deeper themes for speculation. His eye rests upon the 'feeble and ghastly invalids, upon whom death had placed a sure hand, and who sidled and tottered through the mob'. As the night deepens around him the narrator is confronted with a vision that may well have inspired Baudelaire to write 'Les Sept Vieillards' ('Seven Old Men') some nineteen years later. In Poe's tale an old man of some sixty-five or seventy years of age passes by the window and the narrator is struck by what he sees as a figure of 'vast mental power, of caution, of penuriousness, of avarice, of coolness, of malice, of blood-thirstiness, of triumph, of merriment, of excessive terror, of intense – of supreme despair'. Overwhelmed by a curiosity, a 'compelling, irresistible passion', he rushes out of the café to pursue the man.

In 'The Painter of Modern Life' Baudelaire's appreciation of the drawings of Constantin Guys, the Dutch-born illustrator for British and French newspapers, had brought into focus that 'The crowd is his domain' and his admiration for the artist's work was based upon this recognition that Guys's home is a 'dwelling in the throng, in the ebb and flow, the bustle, the fleeting and the infinite'. It is perhaps this interest which later became highlighted by Arnold Hauser when he brought attention to Impressionism's concern for an urban style which describes the 'changeability, the nervous rhythm, the sudden sharp but always ephemeral impressions of the city', anticipating Turnell's suggestion that Baudelaire had succeeded 'better than any other modern poet in conveying the atmosphere of the great city – the mists rising over the Seine at dawn, the sun beating remorselessly down on the dry dusty pavements at noon, and the winter fogs blotting out the sky at dusk; the sinister procession of beggars, murderers, drunkards, prostitutes, and rag-pickers slinking through the twilight'.

The weeping sense of loss felt by the poet in a post-lapsarian world is highlighted in 'The Swan', where the Trojan widow Andromache has lost her own world with Hector, to be brought captive to the world of the invader Neoptolemos (Pyrrhus). Her memory of the Trojan river Simoïs is mimicked in an imitation river with which she is confronted in the land of her imprisonment, a stream fed with her own tears. In Baudelaire's poem the swan bathes in the dust as it cries from 'from deep within lost memory's lake'. Bringing this loss of the past into a modern setting we are presented with glimpses of transience as the 'vieux faubourgs', those 'old neighbourhoods', become the confusion and shapeless indifference of modern Paris. In a similar way the past, the lost, intrudes upon the present in the figures of 'Skeletons at Work' based upon the poet's chance discovery of a print in a neglected book. The figures here are caught in the middle of strenuous and unremitting effort – the articulations of the spine are visible and straining – and far from being patient and long-suffering figures they are instead nightmarish and fearful, caught in the apprehension of mortality. Baudelaire addresses our common experiences with a clear directness as he tells us that 'No promised rest is sure' and we all have some weary and reluctant wakefulness to bring to those lines!

Many of the poems in this sequence possess the sharpness and intensity of a dream, a *dédoublement*, enabling us to contemplate life in a manner that merges the fantastic and the sordidly realistic. Given this, it is no mere chance that the seventeenth poem in the sequence should be dedicated to Constantin Guys and it opens with 'a terrifying landscape' that melts into distance. In this 'Rêve Parisien', this 'Parisian Dream', the poet seems trapped within a world that offers an echo of Piranesi as 'a crazy Tower of Babel' is constituted of stairways and arches containing a 'never-ending palace'. That picture of the poet's garret which had prompted a vision of eternity gazing down over the city in the first poem has now become something new, a terrifying awareness of how soundless eternity stretches out before him.

Ian Brinton,
May 2020

I. Paysage

Je veux, pour composer chastement mes églogues,
Coucher auprès du ciel, comme les astrologues,
Et, voisin des clochers, écouter en rêvant
Leurs hymnes solennels emportés par le vent.
Les deux mains au menton, du haut de ma mansarde,
Je verrai l'atelier qui chante et qui bavarde;
Les tuyaux, les clochers, ces mâts de la cité,
Et les grands ciels qui font rêver d'éternité.

Il est doux, à travers les brumes, de voir naître
L'étoile dans l'azur, la lampe à la fenêtre,
Les fleuves de charbon monter au firmament
Et la lune verser son pâle enchantement.
Je verrai les printemps, les étés, les automnes;
Et quand viendra l'hiver aux neiges monotones,
Je fermerai partout portières et volets
Pour bâtir dans la nuit mes féeriques palais.
Alors je rêverai des horizons bleuâtres,
Des jardins, des jets d'eau pleurant dans les albâtres,
Des baisers, des oiseaux chantant soir et matin,
Et tout ce que l'Idylle a de plus enfantin.
L'Émeute, tempêtant vainement à ma vitre,
Ne fera pas lever mon front de mon pupitre;
Car je serai plongé dans cette volupté
D'évoquer le Printemps avec ma volonté,
De tirer un soleil de mon coeur, et de faire
De mes pensers brûlants une tiède atmosphère.

I. Landscape

For John James

In order to pen my pastoral poems true
I place my couch beneath the stars as fortune-tellers do:
Close neighbour of the clock-towers I muse
On solemn sounds carried on the wind.
Chin resting in both hands, from attic heights
I overlook the singing workshop buzz,
Chimney-pots, bell-towers, the city's masts
To gaze at the sky's ocean, prompting visions of eternity.

Sweet it is through mist to watch the birth of star
Through blue, a lamp lit in a window,
The hearth's ribbons of smoke climbing upwards
And the spilling of the moon's pale wonder.
I shall observe the passing of the seasons
And when the white sheets of winter's snow arrive
Will shutter up the doors
To weave my pleasure-dome within.
My dreaming shall be of distant blue,
Of gardens, water threading its channel through
Alabaster forms; of kisses and of constant birdsong,
Background to childhood's Eden.
Turmoil from the street will vainly knock my window pane,
Not rousing my head from my desk
For I shall be submerged in pleasure
Tracing springtime with my desire,
Kindling sunshine from within and
Warming my world with burning thought.

II. Le Soleil

Le long du vieux faubourg, où pendent aux masures
Les persiennes, abri de secrètes luxures,
Quand le soleil cruel frappe à traits redoublés
Sur la ville et les champs, sur les toits et les blés,
Je vais m'exercer seul à ma fantasque escrime,
Flairant dans tout les coins les hasards de la rime,
Trébuchant sur les mots comme sur les pavés,
Heurtant parfois des vers depuis longtemps rêvés.

Ce père nourricier, ennemi des chloroses,
Éveille dans les champs les vers comme les roses;
I fait s'évaporer les soucis vers le ciel,
Et remplit les cerveaux et les ruches de miel.
C'est lui qui rajeunit les porteurs de béquilles
Et les rends gais et doux comme des jeunes filles,
Et commande aux moissons de croître et de mûrir
Dans le coeur immortel qui toujours veut fleurir!

Quand, ainsi qu'un poëte, il descend dans les villes,
Il ennoblit le sort des choses les plus viles,
Et s'introduit en roi, sans bruit et sans valets,
Dans tous les hôpitaux et dans tous les palais.

II. The Eye of Day

Threading the streets of old suburbs
Where blinds hang over eyes of rotting houses,
Those dwellings of secret lust,
A merciless sun beats and beats again
On town, pasture, roofs and fields of corn;
I weave fantastic on the piste
Pricking out a rhyme from every corner,
Tripping on the cobbles of the words,
Blinded on occasion by verses
Glimpsed elsewhere in my dreams.

That golden ball, enemy of the vapid,
Is father to the worm as well as rose;
He melts our cares in brightness
And brims our brains and hives with honey sweet.
He makes the limp to jump and laugh like girls
And bids the crops burst into ripeness
In an ever-fertile flowering of the heart.

In imitation of the poet he condescends to shed a light
On the fate of darkest corners:
Royally he enters, noiseless and without fuss,
Shedding rays in hospitals and palaces alike.

III. A Une Mendiante Rousse

Blanche fille aux cheveux roux,
Dont la robe par ses trous
Laisse voir la pauvreté
   Et la beauté,

Pour moi, poëte chétif,
Ton jeune corps maladif,
Plein de taches de rousseur,
   A sa douceur.

Tu portes plus galamment
Qu'une reine de roman
Ses cothurnes de velours
   Tes sabots lourds.

Au lieu d'un haillon trop court,
Qu.un superbe habit de cour
Traîne à plis bruyants et longs
   Sur les talons;

En place de bas troués,
Que pour les yeux des roués
Sur ta jambe un poignard d'or
   Reluise encor;

Que de noeuds mal attachés
Dévoilent pour nos péchés
Tes deux beaux seins, radieux
   Comme des yeux;

Que pour te déshabiller
Tes bras se fassent prier
Et chassent à coups mutins
   Les doigts lutins,

III. Redhead on the Streets

Rents in the dress
Of a red-head on the streets
Leak glimpses of poverty
And glamour;

For me, the down-trod poet,
Your sickly frame
Of ruddy blotches
Is offering delight;

Higher classed than heroine
Who sports her velvet fictions
You clatter onwards
In your clogs;

Rather than decked in scanty rags
I should prefer you robed in style
And rustling gowns
Tumbling to your feet;

I would replace your threadbare stockings,
A tease for dirty eyes,
With golden blades
Glinting on your legs;

May a carelessly laced-up bodice
Flaunt, for our lusts,
The beauty of your breasts
Echoing your eyes;

May your flirtatious arms
Refuse to disrobe you,
Tapping and tutting
At mischievous fingers

Perles de la plus belle eau,
Sonnets de maître Belleau
Par tes galants mis au fers
   Sans cesse offerts,

Valetaille de rimeurs
Te dédiant leurs primeurs
Et contemplant ton soulier
   Sous l'escalier,

Maint page épris du hazard,
Maint seigneur et maint Ronsard
Épieraient pour le déduit
   Ton frais réduit!

Tu compterais dans tes lits
Plus de baisers que de lis
Et rangerais sous tes lois
   Plus d'un Valois!

Cependant tu vas gueusant
Quelque vieux débris gisant
Au seuil de quelque Véfour
   De carrefour;

Tu vas lorgnant en dessous
Des bijoux de vingt-neuf sous
Dont je ne puis, oh! pardon!
   Te faire don.

Va donc, sans autre ornament,
Parfum, perles, diamant,
Que ta maigre nudité,
   O ma beauté!

And the pearls of words
Laid down in Bellau's lines
Sent to you by your slavish lovers
Day on day on day,

The first-fruits of the virgin-
Rhymsters dedicating gush
In contemplation of your slipper
From below;

Many a young thruster pierced by Cupid,
Lots of Ronsards, lots of roués,
Would love to peek
Into your young cubby-hole!

You can make a greater tally
Of the kisses not the lilies in your bed
And play the young governess
To more than one toff!

But for now off you go
Begging any old scraps
Round the back of
The high-street bistro;

You gaze longingly
At the imitation jewellery
I cannot afford to buy you
For nothing in return.

Step out then without
Scent, pearls or diamonds,
Decked in skinny nakedness
O my Aphrodite!

IV. Le Cygne

A Victor Hugo

I

Andromaque, je pense à vous! Ce petit fleuve,
Pauvre et triste miroir où jadis resplendit
L'immense majesté de vos douleurs de veuve,
Ce Simoïs menteur qui par vos pleurs grandit,

A fécondé soudain ma mémoire fertile,
Comme je traversais le nouveau Carrousel.
Le vieux Paris n'est plus (la forme d'une ville
Change plus vite, hélas! que le coeur d'un mortel);

Je ne vois qu'en esprit tout ce camp de baraques,
Ces tas de chapiteaux ébauchés et de fûts,
Les herbes, les gros blocs verdis par l'eau des flaques,
Et, brillant aux carreaux, le bric-à-brac confus.

Là s'étalait jadis une ménagerie;
Là je vis, un matin, à l'heure où sous les cieux
Froids et clairs le Travail s'éveille, où la voirie
Pousse un sombre ouragan dans l'air silencieux,

Un cygne qui s'était évadé de sa cage,
Et, de ses pieds palmés frottant le pavé sec,
Sur le sol raboteaux traînait son blanc plumage.
Près d'un ruisseau sans eau la bête ouvrant le bec

Baignait nerveusement ses ailes dans la poudre,
Et disait, le coeur plein de son beau lac natal:
"Eau, quand donc pleuvras-tu? quand tonneras-tu, foudre?"
Je vois ce malheureux, mythe étrange et fatal,

Vers le ciel quelquefois, comme l'homme d'Ovide,
Vers le ciel ironique et cruellement bleu,
Sur son cou convulsif tendant sa tête avide,
Comme s'il adressait des reproches à Dieu!

IV. The Swan

To Victor Hugo

I

Andromache, you occupy my mind! This little trickle,
A thin and sad enduring of what yesterday reflected
The enormous majesty of your widow's weeds,
Faithless Simoïs, whose first false words were swollen

With your tears of loss, has bubbled up again into my mind
As I made a crossing of the newly laid-out Carrousel.
The old city is gone now, shifting faster than a human heart,
And old Paris can no more be found;

It's only when I shut my eyes that I can bring to life
Again those stalls, those heaps of stone capitals,
Fragments of pillars, weeds springing between blocks
Of greened stone, jumbled goods in shop-fronts.

Beneath the cold clear sky of work-place dawn,
Amid the bin-men's clatter through the stillness,
In my mind's eye recalling where
Once a zoo had been, I saw

A swan that had escaped from being shuttered up,
Slapping its webbed feet along dry pavements
And trailing white plumage through the dirt.
Beside a dried-up stream its beak hung open

As it vainly flapped its wings stirring dust
And cried from deep within lost memory's lake:
"Water, when will you return? Thunder storm again?"
I see this doom-laden exile

Snaking its drought-struck throat upwards
At a blue and heartless sky
As if to screech from Ovid's tales
Reproach aimed at the gates of God.

II

Paris change! mais rien dans ma mélancolie
N'a bougé! palais neufs, échafaudages, blocs,
Vieux faubourgs, tout pour moi devient allégorie,
Et mes chers souvenirs sont plus lourds que des rocs.

Aussi devant ce Louvre une image m'opprime:
Je pense à mon grand cygne, avec ses gestes fous,
Comme les exilés, ridicule et sublime,
Et rongé d'un désir sans trêve! et puis à vous,

Andromaque, des bras d'un grand époux tombée,
Vil bétail, sous la main du superbe Pyrrhus,
Auprès d'un tombeau vide en extase courbée;
Veuve d'Hector, hélas! et femme d'Hélénus!

Je pense à la négresse, amaigrie et phthisique,
Piétinant dans la boue, et cherchant, l'oeil hagard,
Les cocotiers absents de la superbe Afrique
Derrière la muraille immense du brouillard;

A quiconque a perdu ce qui ne se retrouve
Jamais, jamais! à ceux qui s'abreuvent de pleurs
Et tettent la Douleur comme une bonne louve!
Aux maigres orphelins séchant comme des fleurs!

Ainsi dans la forêt où mon esprit s'exile
Un vieux Souvenir sonne à plein souffle du cor!
Je pense aux matelots oubliés dans une île,
Aux captifs, aux vaincus!...à bien d'autres encor!

II

Paris is changing yet nothing in my melancholy mind
Shifts; scaffolding rises, new buildings, old neighbourhoods,
Metamorphosis before my eyes; my dearest
Recollections sit like stone.

In front of the Louvre Palace an image weighs me down:
I think of my fine swan of frantic gesture,
Marginal and foolish like an exile,
Devoured by unrequited longing and then

I think of you, Andromache, toppled
From a mighty husband's clasp into the gated livestock pen
Of Pyrrhus; winged grief outside an empty tomb;
Widow of Hector, wife of Helenus.

I think then of the negress, emaciated and wheezing,
Stumbling through mud, searching for the coconut palms
Of Africa but with eyes walled in
By the unending prison of fog;

And then of those who have lost what will never return,
Who sate their thirst on tears and suck
The she-wolf's tit of pain;
Of undernourished orphans whose roots are drying out.

Adrift in endless forests of my exiled soul
An ancient thought winds its distant horn
As I think of stranded sailors on a shore,
Of prisoners, defeated...and many others more.

V. Les Sept Vieillards

Fourmillante cité, cité pleine de rêves,
Où le spectre en plein jour raccroche le passant!
Les mystères partout coulent comme des séves
Dans les canaux étroits du colosse puissant.

Un matin, cependant que dans la triste rue
Les maisons, dont la brume allongeait la hauteur,
Simulaient les deux quais d'une rivière accrue,
Et que, décor semblable à l'âme de l'acteur,

Un brouillard sale et jaune inondait tout l'espace,
Je suivais, roidissant mes nerfs comme un héros
Et discutant avec mon âme déjà lasse,
Le faubourg secoué par les lourds tombereaux.

Tout à coup, un vieillard dont les guenilles jaunes
Imitaient la couleur de ce ciel pluvieux,
Et dont l'aspect aurait fait pleuvoir les aumônes,
Sans la méchanceté qui luisait dans ses yeux,

M'apparut. On eût dit sa prunelle trempée
Dans le fiel; son regard aiguisait les frimas,
Et sa barbe à longs poils, roide comme une épée,
Se projetait, pareille à celle de Judas.

Il n'était pas voûté, mais cassé, son échine
Faisant avec sa jambe un parfait angle droit,
Si bien que son bâton, parachevant sa mine,
Lui donnait la tournure et le pas maladroit

D'un quadrupède infirme ou d'un juif à trois pattes.
Dans la neige et la boue il allait s'empêtrant,
Comme s'il écrasait des morts sous ses savates,
Hostile à l'univers plutôt qu'indifférent.

V. Seven Old Men

Seething city anthill bursting with dreams
Where ghouls in broad daylight accost the passer-by!
Life's eerie sap trickles the length
Of the narrow waterways of this pulsing giant.

One morning, whilst the houses
Distorted in height by shimmering mist
Appeared like stone shores of a swelling river
And a filthy yellow fog garbed an actor's soul

To overwhelm the world,
I, with nerves pitch wrought, wound
Through suburbs of throbbing hearses
That chattered to my laden soul.

All at once an ancient man in yellowed rags,
The shade akin to damp skyscape,
Whose features would have prompted alms
Were it not for the glint of malice in his eyes

Started up before me with wormwood glance;
His stiletto stare glinted frost
Long bristles of an epée beard
Thrust outward like that of Judas.

His back, more snapped than bent,
Formed a right-angle to the legs
So that his staff, to complete the tripod,
Gave him a jerking, halting step

Like a crippled quadruped or a money-lender
On three stilts scuffling onwards through snow and mud
Grating the dead in his worn-out slippers
With venom more than lack of care.

Son pareil le suivait: barbe, oeil, dos, bâton, loques,
Nul trait ne distinguait, du même enfer venu,
Ce jumeau centenaire, et ces spectres baroques
Marchaient du même pas vers un but inconnu.

A quel complot infâme étais-je donc en butte,
Ou quel méchant hasard ainsi m'humiliait?
Car je comptai sept fois, de minute en minute,
Ce sinistre vieillard qui se multipliait!

Que celui-là qui rit de mon inquiétude,
Et qui n'est pas saisi d'un frisson fraternel,
Songe bien que malgré tant de décrépitude
Ces sept monstres hideux avaient l'air éternel!

Aurais-je, sans mourir, contemplé le huitième,
Sosie inexorable, ironique et fatal,
Dégoûtant Phénix, fils et père de lui-même?
—Mais je tournai le dos au cortége infernal.

Exaspéré comme un ivrogne qui voit double,
Je rentrai, je fermai ma porte, épouvanté,
Malade et morfondu, l'esprit fiévreux et trouble,
Blessé par le mystère et par l'absurdité!

Vainement ma raison voulait prendre la barre;
La tempête en jouant déroutait ses efforts,
Et mon âme dansait, dansait, vieille gabarre
Sans mâts, sur une mer monstrueuse et sans bords!

His double shuffled on behind, beard and eye,
Back, staff and rags, a duplicate exiting from Hell,
An ancient twin mirroring his steps
Towards some unknown rendezvous.

What dreadful trick is being played me
What wicked game to make me feel a fool?
From minute to minute I ticked off
Seven replicas of this sinister old man!

Before you laugh at my rising panic
To distance yourself from a neighbourly shudder
Consider well how these seven vile apparitions
Carried a sense of the eternal within their forms.

Could I have gazed upon an eighth and lived,
Gazed upon a further fatal double,
Foul Phoenix, son and father all the same?
– I turned my back on this cortège from Hell.

Self-doubting like a drunk who sees things double
I stumbled home and slammed my door,
Sick, bewildered to my core, wounded
By the ridiculous absurd.

My common sense tried to take a grip
But the banging winds destabilised my world
Leaving my mind to rock back and forth
Rudderless on a monstrous empty sea!

VI. Les Petites Vieilles

A Victor Hugo

I

Dans les plis sinueux des vieilles capitales,
Où tout, même l'horreur, tourne aux enchantements,
Je guette, obéissant à mes humeurs fatales,
Des êtres singuliers, décrepits et charmants.

Ces monstres disloqués furent jadis des femmes,
Éponine ou Laïs! Monstres brisés, bossus
Ou tordus, aimons-les! ce sont encor des âmes.
Sous des jupons troués et sous de froids tissus

Ils rampant, flagellés par les bises iniques,
Frémissant au fracas roulant des omnibus,
Et serrant sur leur flanc, ainsi que des reliques,
Un petit sac brodé de fleurs ou de rébus;

Ils trottent, tout pareils à des marionettes;
Se traînent, comme font les animaux blessés,
Ou dansent, sans vouloir danser, pauvres sonnettes
Où se pend un Démon sans pitié! Tout cassés

Qu'ils sont, ils ont des yeux perçants comme une vrille,
Luisants comme ces trous où l'eau dort dans la nuit;
Ils ont les yeux divins de la petite fille
Qui s'étonne et qui rit à tout ce qui reluit.

—Avez-vous observé que maints cercueils de vieilles
Sont presque aussi petits que celui d'un enfant?
La Mort savante met dans ces bières pareilles
Un symbole d'un goût bizarre et captivant,

Et lorsque j'entrevois un fantôme débile
Traversant de Paris le fourmillant tableau,
Il me semble toujours que cet être fragile
S'en va tout doucement vers un nouveau berceau;

VI. Little Old Ladies

For Victor Hugo

I

In the pleated windings of the old town
Where even destitution is touched by magic
I focus my attention, as if by magnetic impulse,
On faded, tattered charmers!

I sing the lay of dislocated freaks, once so feminine,
Some Éponine or Laïs now round-shouldered,
Scarred and crumpled, disguising someone real.
Beneath torn skirts and lacy satin

They totter, whipped by sharp winds
And shiver at the shattering din of passing buses
And clutch to their bosoms their holy relics,
Their little handbags decked with flowers or runes;

They simper by like puppets on a string;
They hobble like a wounded creature
Compelled to jig like a bell's tongue
Jerked by an unforgiving demon! Crumpled

Though they may be but mascara glintings
Surface from the darkness of the wells
And little girly glances
Are conjured by laughter and by light.

Have you ever taken note of how coffins
Of the old are shrunken small like coffins of the young?
Shrewd old death reveals symbolic likenesses
With this intriguing parallel

And when confronted by a feeble spectre
Drifting through the swarming Paris streets
I always glimpse a tattered doll
Heading quietly for a second childhood;

A moins que, méditant sur la géométrie,
Je ne cherche, à l'aspect de ces membres discords,
Combien de fois il faut que l'ouvrier varie
La forme de la boîte où l'on met tous ces corps.

—Ces yeux sont des puits faits d'un million de larmes,
Des creusets qu'un métal refroidi pailleta...
Ces yeux mystérieux ont d'invincibles charmes
Pour celui que l'austère Infortune allaita !

Or, reflecting upon the geometric progress
Of such shuffling limbs I often wonder
How many times the coffin-maker has to redesign
The box in which to cram such corpses.

– Those deep dark wells are filled with countless tears,
Sequins glinting in metal troughs,
Mysterious eyes of seductive charm
For whoever nuzzled misfortune's breast.

II

De Frascati défunt Vestale enamourée;
Prêtresse de Thalie, hélas! dont le souffleur
Enterré sait le nom; célèbre évaporée
Ques Tivoli jadis ombragea dans sa fleur,

Toutes m'enivrent! Mais parmi ces êtres frêles
Il en est qui, faisant de la douleur un miel,
Ont dit au Dévouement qui leur prêtait ses ailes:
Hippogriffe puissant, mène-moi jusqu'au ciel!

L'une, par sa patrie au malheur exercée,
L'autre, que son époux surchargea de douleurs,
L'autre, par son enfant Madone transpercée,
Toutes auraient pu faire un fleuve avec leurs pleurs!

III

Ah! que j'en ai suivi de ces petites vieilles!
Une, entre autres, à l'heure où le soleil tombant
Ensanglante le ciel de blessures vermeilles,
Pensive, s'asseyait à l'écart sur un banc,

Pour entendre un de ces concerts, riches de cuivre,
Dont les soldats parfois inondent nos jardins,
Et qui, dans ces soirs d'or où l'on se sent revivre,
Versent quelque héroïsme au coeur des citadins.

Celle-là, droite encore, fière et sentant la règle,
Humait avidement ce chant vif et guerrier;
Son oeil parfois s'ouvrait comme l'oeil d'un vieil aigle;
Son front de marbre avait l'air fait pour le laurier!

II

The revered favourite of some long-dead Frascati;
Some priestess of Thalia whose name was only known
To some long-dead prompter; some great figure
Known in her prime at the Tivoli but now long gone,

The scent of them all blurs my senses as among these
Delicate memories lie those whose anguish turned to honey
Addressing the 'Devotion' which set them soaring:
Oh Hippogriff work once more for me!

One whose native world schooled her in torment,
And another whose husband weighed her down in pain
A third compelled by her son to feel a Madonna's sorrow
All could feed a river with their tears!

III

How my mind has traced and tracked those ladies!
One comes to mind, sitting alone on a park bench
Pensive as the setting sun slashes
Red a wounded sky;

She listens to a brass-band concert
Overwhelm the civic garden
As the evening settles down in gold
And heroism fills dwellers to the brim.

Pride makes her sit stiff upright in response,
Attentive to the lively strains of glory,
Open-eyed old eagle on a crag
With marble forehead fit for a laurel crown!

IV

Tells vous cheminez, stoïques et sans plaintes,
A travers le chaos des vivantes cités,
Mères au coeur saignant, courtisanes ou saintes,
Dont autrefois les noms par tous étaient cités.

Vous qui fûtes la grâce ou qui fûtes la gloire,
Nul ne vous reconnaît! un ivrogne incivil
Vous insulte en passant d'un amour dérisoire;
Sur vos talons gambade un enfant lâche et vil.

Honteuses d'exister, ombres tatatinées,
Peureuses, le dos bas, vous côtoyez les murs;
Et nul ne vous salue, étranges destinées!
Débris d'humanité pour l'éternité mûrs!

Mais moi, moi qui de loin tendrement vous surveille,
L'oeil inquiet, fixé sur vos pas incertains,
Tout comme si j'étais votre père, ô merveille!
Je goûte à votre insu des plaisirs clandestins:

Je vois s'épanouir vos passions novices;
Sombres ou lumineux, je vis vos jours perdus;
Mon coeur multiplié jouit de tous vos vices!
Mon âme respendit de toutes vos vertus!

Ruines! ma famille! ô cerveaux congénères!
Je vous fais chaque soir un solennel adieu!
Où serez-vous demain, Èves octogénaires,
Sur qui pèse la griffe effroyable de Dieu?

IV

And so you wind your way through the confusion
Of the swarming city, patient and uncomplaining,
Whores and saints, mothers of the bleeding heart
Whose names were once upon the lips of all.

You whose grace and style were once the hallmark
Are recognised no longer; an ill-mannered drunk
Insults you with an exaggerated pass
Or an urchin off the street kicks your heels!

Clinging hunched and close to the wall in fear,
These wizened shades hug their years in shame;
Addressed by no one, having drifted beyond their time,
Wreckage of humanity on the verge of the next move!

But with a tender and an anxious glance
I still watch you tottering on your paths,
As if you were my children who little knew
How proudly I took pleasure in your world.

Watching your new little tricks, in darkness or in light,
I allow my eye to roam over your long gone days;
My heart springs with joy at all your vices!
My soul glows bright in response to your virtues!

My family in ruins, blood of the same blood,
I bid you every night a solemn adieu!
Where will you be tomorrow, my ageing Eves,
As God's terrifying claw is poised above your skulls?

VII. Les Aveugles

Contemples-les, mon âme; ils sont vraiment affreux!
Pareils aux mannequins; vaguement ridicules;
Terribles, singuliers comme les somnambules;
Dardant on ne sait où leurs globes ténébreux.

Leurs yeux, d'où la divine étincelle est partie,
Comme s'ils regardaient au loin, restent levés
Au ciel; on ne les voit jamais vers les pavés
Pencher rêveusement leur tête appesantie.

Ils traversent ainsi le noir illimité,
Ce frère du silence éternal. O cité!
Pendant qu'autour de nous tu chantes, ris et beugles,

Éprise du plaisir jusqu'à l'atrocité,
Vois! je me traîne aussi! mais, plus qu'eux hébété,
Je dis: Que cherchent-ils au Ciel, tous ces aveugles?

VII. The Blind

Let my mind focus upon the truly frightful!
Imitations of shop-window dummies;
Individual and shocking, like walking corpses
They dart blank eyes to and fro.

Those eyes from which the sparkle has long vanished
Lock on distances, staring skywards;
You'll never see them meditate on
Pavement slabs beneath their feet.

They voyage through an endless night
Blood brothers to noiseless death.
The city round us sings, laughs and howls

Trapped in ferocious pleasuring;
Behold me, stumbling on, more self-enclosed than the blind,
Muttering what do the dead stare at in the sky?

VIII. A Une Passante

La rue assourdissante autour de moi hurlait.
Longue, mince, en grand deuil, douleur majestueuse,
Une femme passa, d'une main fasteuse
Soulevant, balançant le feston et l'ourlet;

Agile et noble, avec sa jambe de statue.
Moi, je buvais, crispé comme un extravagant,
Dans son oeil, ciel livide où germe l'ouragan,
La douceur qui fascine et le plaisir qui tue.

Un éclair...puis la nuit!—Fugitive beauté
Dont le regard m'a fait soudainement renaître,
Ne te verrai-je plus que dans l'éternité?

Ailleurs, bien loin d'ici! trop tard! *jamais* peut-être!
Car j'ignore où tu fuis, tu ne sais où je vais,
O toi que j'eusse aimée, ô toi qui le savais!

VIII. A Passerby

Inside the deafening roar of streets around me
A tall, slim woman in widow's weeds stepped by;
With lavish gesture this Queen of Grief
Raised the hem and bunches of her dress:

Supple and majestic with marble limb.
Tense, like a man struck, I drank deeply
From her glance: a whitened sky that comes before a storm;
A softness which bewitches; a pleasure linked with death.

A flash...then darkness! That beauty of the instant
Whose look has shocked me back into this life
Shall I catch a glimpse again this side of eternity?

Some other time or place! Too late and maybe never!
I do not know your pathway and you certainly know not mine:
You who could have held my love; you who knew that too!

IX. Le Squelette Laboureur

I

Dans les planches d'anatomie
Qui traînent sur ces quais poudreux
Où maint livre cadavéreux
Dort comme une antique momie,

Dessins auxquels la gravité
Et le savoir d'un vieil artiste,
Bien que le sujet en soit triste,
Ont communiqué la Beauté,

On voit, ce qui rend plus complètes
Ces mystérieuses horreurs,
Bêchant comme des laboureurs,
Des Écorchès et des Squelettes.

II

De ce terrain que vous fouillez,
Manants résignés et funebres,
De tout l'effort de vos vertèbres,
Ou de vos muscles dépouillés,

Dites, quelle moisson étrange,
Forçats arrachés au charnier,
Tirez-vous, et de quel fermier
Avez-vous à remplir la grange?

Voulez-vous (d'un destin trop dur
Épouvantable et clair emblème!)
Montrer que dans la fosse même
Le sommeil promis n'est pas sûr;

IX. Skeleton at Work

I

Amongst those illustrations from anatomy
That lie boxed along the dusty quay-side
Where many ancient books
Rest sleeping in their antique tombs

Are drawings reflecting the gravitas
And academic knowledge of an old master
Who created Beauty
From a subject deeply sad

To make us see a wholeness
Of mysterious horror,
A skeleton work-force
Digging like workmen on the land.

II

From the clods which you turn over,
Patient and mournful villeins,
With the straining backbone effort
Of your knots of bony muscle

Tell me what strange crop
You are condemned to wrest from the grave
And whose silo are you
Compelled to fill?

Are you there to show us a clear picture
Of terrifying destiny
Where even in the cemetery
No promised rest is sure;

Qu'envers nous le Néant est traître;
Que tout, même la Mort, nous ment,
Et que sempiternellement,
Hélas! il nous faudra peut-être

Dans quelque pays inconnu
Écorcher la terre revêche
Et pousser une lourde bêche
Sous notre pied sanglant et nu?

That even nothingness deceives
That even Death gives us the lie,
And that throughout Eternity,
Alas, we are perhaps constrained

In some unknown country
To turn the sods of sullen ground
By driving down a heavy spade
Beneath our blood-soaked naked foot?

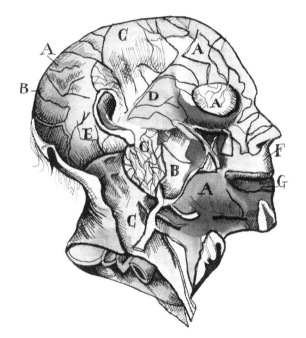

Anatomie, Arteres de la face

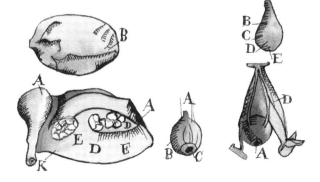

X. Le Crépuscule du Soir

Voici le soir charmant, ami du criminal;
Il vient comme un complice, à pas de loup; le ciel
Se ferme lentement comme une grande alcôve,
Et l'homme impatient se change en bête fauve.

O soir, amiable soir, désiré par celui
Dont les bras, sans mentir, peuvent dire: Aujourd'hui
Nous avons travaillé!—C'est le soir qui soulage
Les esprits que dévore une douleur sauvage,
Le savant obstiné dont le front s'alourdit,
Et l'ouvrier courbé qui regagne son lit.
Cependant des démons malsains dans l'atmosphère
S'éveillent lourdement, comme des gens d'affaire,
Et cognent en volant les volets et l'auvent.
A travers les lueurs que tourmente le vent
La Prostitution s'allume dans les rues;
Comme une fourmillière elle ouvre ses issues;
Partout elle se fraye un occulte chemin,
Ainsi que l'ennemi qui tente un coup de main;
Elle remue au sein de la cité de fange
Comme un ver qui dérobe a l'Homme ce qu'il mange.

On entend çà et là les cuisines siffler,
Les théâtres glapir, les orchestres ronfler;
Les tables d'hôte, dont le jeu fait les délices,
S'emplissent de catins et d'escrocs, leur complices,
Et les voleurs, qui n'ont ni trêve ni merci,
Vont bientôt commencer leur travail, eux aussi,
Et forcer doucement les portes et les caisses
Pour vivre quelques jours et vêtir leurs maîtresses.

Recueille-toi, mon âme, en ce grave moment,
Et ferme ton oreille à ce rugissement.
C'est l'heure où les douleurs des malades s'aigrissent!
Le sombre Nuit les prend à la gorge; ils finissent
Leur destinée et vont vers le gouffre commun;
L'hôpital se remplit de leurs soupirs.—Plus d'un

X. Nightfall

The charm of evening, friend to the criminal,
Arrives on time like an accomplice with wolf's stealth;
The sky slowly lowers to form an abyss
And the eager man transforms into savage beast.

Welcome evening sought for by those who can in truth assert:
"We've done some work today!"
Evening that offers solace to those consumed by grief,
Those persevering scholars whose heads begin to nod,
Those bowed workmen who return to lie down.
Meanwhile infected devils in the air rouse
Slowly like men of business who fly past
To rap on shutters and on porches.
Beneath the light of gas-lamps flickering in the wind
Prostitution comes to life in the streets
As if passages from an anthill are now thrown open
Spawning a mysterious pathway to an enemy
Who baits the trap; it beckons from the heart of filth
Like a worm that steals food from a man's mouth.

From here and there the hiss of kitchens,
The yap from theatres, the deep sound of orchestras;
The evening set-menus with gambling for dessert,
Home to harlots, swindlers and their lackeys;
The thieves who don't think twice prepare to get to work,
Softly forcing doors and safes,
To get the cash to live and dress their trollops.

Let my mind retreat at this grave hour
And shut my ears to such a din.
This is the time when the pain of illness sharpens!
Darkness has its fingers at their throats
As their time is up and they shuffle towards the common pit;
The hospital gasps out their sighs.
More than one will not return to sit and sup

Ne viendra plus chercher la soupe parfumée,
Au coin du feu, le soir, auprès d'une âme aimée.

Encore la plupart n'ont-ils jamais connu
La douceur du foyer et n'ont jamais vécu!

Close to the fire of an evening, beside a loved one.

Most of them have never known indeed
The quiet of a domestic hearth: most have never lived!

XI. Le Jeu

Dans les fauteuils fanés des courtisanes vieilles,
Pâles, le sourcil peint, l'oeil câlin et fatal,
Minaudant, et faisant de leurs maigres oreilles
Tomber un cliquetis de pierre et de métal;

Autour des verts tapis des visages sans lèvre,
Des lèvres sans couleur, des mâchoires sans dent,
Et des doigts convulsés d'une infernale fièvre,
Fouillant la poche vide ou le sein palpitant;

Sous de sales plafonds un rang de pâles lustres
Et d'énormes quinquets projetant leurs lueurs
Sur des fronts ténébreux de poëtes illustres
Qui viennent gaspiller leurs sanglantes sueurs;

Voilà le noir tableau qu'en un rêve nocturne
Je vis se dérouler sous mon oeil clairvoyant.
Moi-même, dans un coin de l'antre taciturne,
Je me vis accoudé, froid, muet, enviant,

Enviant de ces gens la passion tenace,
De ces vieilles putains la funèbre gaieté,
Et tous gaillardement trafiquant à ma face,
L'un de son vieil honneur, l'autre de sa beauté!

Et mon coeur s'effraya d'envier maint pauvre homme
Courant avec ferveur a l'abîme béant,
Et qui, soûl de son sang, préférait en somme
La douleur à la mort et l'enfer au néant!

XI. The Gaming-Room

With pencilled eyebrows over lethal eyes,
Jaundiced old whores settle in faded armchairs;
They simper and rattle a clink of stone and metal
Which dangles from their withered ears.

Faces without lips, lips without colour, jaws without teeth
Are ranged around the tables of green baize
Whilst jiggling fingers root
Round empty pockets and breasts shudder from side to side.

Beneath the filthy ceilings chandeliers in a line
Cast their dim light upon the shadowed brows
Of poets of renown who come
To squander their hard-won talents.

In a night-time vision
I saw this bleak canvas unroll before my very eyes
And there was I in a corner of the hushed cave
Chin on hands, cold and tranced in envy

Of the intense commitment of those men
And the lugubrious grins of the old whores
As all swapped and sold before my eyes
Their honour and their beauty!

And my mind trembled to be envying
Such creatures who were hastening to the Pit
Intoxicated by their own passion for pain
Hovering over death and the emptiness of Hell!

XII. Danse Macabre

Fière, autant qu'un vivant, de sa noble stature,
Avec son gros bouquet, son mouchoir et ses gants,
Elle a la nonchalance et la désinvolure
D'une coquette maigre aux airs extravagants.

Vit-on jamais au bal une taille plus mince?
Sa robe exagérée, en sa royale ampleur,
S'écroule abondamment sur un pied sec que pince
Un soulier pomponné, jolie comme une fleur.

La ruche qui se joue au bord des clavicules,
Comme un ruisseau lascif qui se frotte au rocher,
Défend pudiquement des lazzi ridicules
Les funèbres appas qu'elle tient à cacher.

Ses yeux profonds sont faits de vide et de ténèbres,
Et son crâne, de fleurs artistement coiffé,
Oscille mollement sur ses frêles vertèbres,
O charme d'un néant follement attifé!

Aucuns t'appelleront une caricature,
Qui ne comprennent pas, amants ivre de chair,
L'élégance sans nom de l'humaine armature.
Tu réponds, grand squelette, à mon goût le plus cher!

Viens-tu troubler, avec ta puissante grimace,
La fête de la Vie? Ou quelque vieux désir,
Éperonnant encor ta vivante carcasse,
Te pousse-t-il, crédule, au sabbat du Plaisir?

Au chant des violons, aux flammes des bougies,
Espères-tu chasser ton cauchemar moqueur,
Et viens-tu demander au torrent des orgies
De refraîchir l'enfer allumé dans ton coeur?

XII. Death's Jig

Proud of her stately figure, as if she were alive,
She clutches gloves, hanky and full-blown bouquet,
A devil-may-care pose of off-hand ease
And the flamboyant air of the practiced flirt.

What a stream-lined figure at the ball!
The ample folds of flowing dress
Cascade towards a dried-out foot
Trapped in a decorated dancing pump.

Frills rustle on the shores of her collar-bone
Like a bubbling stream nestling around a rock,
Clothing the skeletal charms she strives to hide
From open-mouthed mirth and gibe.

Her eyes are dark and empty pools
And her skull, artfully bewigged with flowers,
Perches nodding on her bony spine.
Mystique of emptiness dressed in trumpery!

Those lovers who become obsessed by flesh
Will dismiss your presence as mere caricature
Without recognising the elegance of your framework:
But you appeal to my dearest needs, skeleton!

Have you brought your powerful grin to disrupt
The mirth of the feast? Or does some shadow of desire
Shudder in your corpse nudging it
To join our Antic Revels?

In flickering candlelight and to the strains of the violin
Are you hoping to disguise the nightmare of that grin?
Are you seeking a cascade of orgy
To drown the throbbing hell within you?

Inépuisable puits de sottise et de fautes!
De l'antique douleur éternel alembic!
A travers le treillis recourbé de tes côtes
Je vois, errant encor, l'insatiable aspic.

Pour dire vrai, je crains que ta coquetterie
Ne trouve pas un prix digne de ses efforts;
Qui, de ces coeurs mortels, entend la raillerie?
Les charmes de l'horreur n'enivrent que les forts!

Le gouffres de tes yeux, plein d'horribles pensées,
Exhale le vertige, et les danseurs prudents
Ne contempleront pas sans d'amères nausées
Le sourire éternel de ses trente-deux dents.

Pourtant, qui n'a serré dans ses bras un squelette,
Et qui ne s'est nourri des choses du tombeau?
Qu'importe le parfum, l'habit ou la toilette?
Qui fait le dégoûté montre qu'il se croit beau.

Bayadère sans nez, irrésistible gouge,
Dis donc à ces danseurs qui font les offusqués:
"Fiers mignons, malgré l'art des poudres et du rouge,
Vous sentez tous la mort! O squelette musqués,

Antinous fletris, dandys à face glabre,
Cadavres vernissés, lovelaces chenus,
Le branle universel et la danse macabre
Vous entraîne en des lieux qui ne sont pas connus!

Des quais froids de la Seine aux bords brûlants du Gange,
Le troupeau mortel saute et se pâme, sans voir
Dans un trou du plafond la trompette de l'Ange
Sinistrement béante ainsi qu'un tremblon noir.

En tout climat, sous tout soleil, la Mort t'admire
En tes contorsions, risible Humanité,
Et souvent, comme toi, se parfumant de myrrhe,
Mêle son ironie à ton insanité!"

Inexhaustible depths of folly and of error!
Everlasting still of ancient suffering!
I watch the ever hungry serpent's threads
Winding through the trellis of your ribs.

To tell the truth, I fear that your flirtations
Will never gain the prize that seems worthy of your efforts;
Can any of these mortals get the joke?
None but the bold accept horror's calling-card!

Provocative of terrifying thoughts
Your hollow eye-sockets make the world reel
And the constant smirk of your thirty-two white teeth
Prompts bile to rise to the dancer's lips.

Yet who has never hugged a skeleton in his grip
And who has never nibbled on the dead?
What is the point of perfume, dress or make-up?
Whoever pretends disgust thinks highly of himself.

Tip-toed glider without a nose, enticing drab,
Go tell those other dancers who put on airs
"You stuck-up darlings, beneath your rouged and powdered cheeks
You stink of mortality! O sweet-scented skeletons,

Withered Antinous, smooth-cheeked fop,
Glossy body of a hoary-headed Lovelace,
The world-wide beat of the Dance of Death
Whirls you beyond the horizon's end.

From the cold Seine quays to the burning shores of Ganges
The human flock jig and jive not taking notice
Of the gaping ceiling through which the Final Trump
Yawns its black throat like a blunderbuss.

Worldwide beneath every sky Death watches
Your writhing, laughable Humanity,
And, like you, she soaks herself with myrrh
Ironically smirking at your madness!"

XIII. L'Amour du Mensonge

Quand je te vois passer, ô ma chère indolente,
Au chant des instruments qui se brise au plafond
Suspendant ton allure harmonieuse et lente,
Et promenant l'ennui de ton regard profond;

Quand je contemple, aux feux du gaz qui le colore,
Ton front pâle, embelli par un morbide attrait,
Où les torches du soir allument une aurore,
Et tes yeux attirants comme ceux d'un portrait,

Je me dis: Qu'elle est belle! Et bizarrement fraîche!
Le souvenir massif, royale et lourde tour,
La couronne, et son coeur, meutri comme une pêche,
Est mûr, comme son corps, pour le savant amour.

Es-tu le fruit d'automne aux saveurs souveraines?
Est-tu vase funèbre attendant quelques pleurs,
Parfum qui fait rêver aux oasis lointaines,
Oreiller caressant, ou corbeille de fleurs?

Je sais qu'il est des yeux, des plus mélancoliques,
Qui ne recèlent point de secrets précieux;
Beaux écrins sans joyaux, médaillons sans reliques,
Plus vides, plus profonds que vous-mêmes, ô Cieux!

Mais ne suffit-il pas que du sois l'apparence,
Pour réjouir un coeur qui fuit la verité?
Qu'importe ta bêtise ou ton indifférence?
Masque ou décor, salut! J'adore ta beauté.

XIII. In Love with Deceit

As I watch you moving by with slothful ease
In time to the music which throbs down from the ceiling
Holding in suspension your harmonious allure
By casting forth indifference from your pools of eyes;

As I gaze upon your white-painted face made life-like
With morbid charm in the flickering of the gas-lamps,
Glimmers of night that bring to mind the dawn,
And your eyes draw me in as with a portrait,

I tell myself how beautiful she is, how full of life!
Vivid memory conjures up a towering regal presence
Built round the bruised peach of a heart
Within a ripeness of a body built for love.

Are you the fruit of autumn's mellow scents?
Are you an urn inviting weeping dedication,
Or perfume weaving an oasis in desert distance,
A soothing cushion or a garland of narcosis?

I know that some most mournful glances
Contain no precious treasures behind the curtain,
Caskets void of jewels, empty tombs
Vaster than the wide expanse of sky!

But isn't your sham surface quite sufficient
To bring joy to a mind that eschews truth?
What matters your stupidity or trivia?
All hail to your appearance! It's your beauty I adore.

XIV. Nostalgie

Je n'ai pas oublié, voisine de la ville,
Notre blanche maison, petite mais tranquille;
Sa Pomone de plâtre et sa vieille Vénus
Dans un bosquet chétif cachant leurs membres nus,
Et le soleil, le soir, ruisselant et superbe,
Qui, derrière la vitre où se brisait sa gerbe,
Semblait, grand oeil ouvert dans le ciel curieux,
Contempler nos dîners longs et silencieux,
Répandant largement ses beaux reflets de cierge
Sur la nappe frugale et les rideaux de serge.

XIV. Nostalgia

I have never lost sight of our small white house
So close to the town; so peaceful
With its plaster casts of Venus and Pomona
Concealing their nudity within a scanty grove of trees
Whilst the evening sun shimmered in pride
Behind the window pane as if its large eye
Stood open in the skies to watch our long and silent dinners
And shed its candle-like reflection on
The cheap table-cloth and curtains of serge.

XV. Mariette

La servante au grand coeur dont vous étiez jalouse,
Et qui dort son sommeil sous une humble pelouse,
Nous devrions pourtant lui porter quelques fleurs.
Les morts, les pauvres morts, ont de grandes douleurs,
Et quand Octobre souffle, émendeur des vieux arbres,
Son vent mélancolique à l'entour de leurs marbres,
Certe, ils doivent trouver les vivants bien ingrats,
A dormir, comme ils font, chaudement dans leurs draps,
Tandis que, dévorés de noires songeries,
Sans compagnon de lit, sans bonnes causeries,
Vieux squelettes gelés travaillés par le ver,
Ils sentent s'égoutter les neiges de l'hiver
Et le siècle couler, sans qu'amis ni famille
Remplacent les lambeaux qui pendent à leur grille.
Lorsque la bûche siffle et chante, si le soir,
Calme, dans le fauteuil je la voyais s'asseoir,
Si, par une nuit bleue et froide de décembre,
Je la trouvais tapie en un coin de ma chambre,
Grave, et venant du fond de son lit éternel
Couver l'enfant grandi de son oeil maternel,
Que pourrais-je répondre à cette âme pieuse,
Voyant tomber des pleurs de sa paupière creuse?

XV. Mariette

I know she made you jealous but we should place some flowers
On that secluded grave where lies beneath the ground
My warm-hearted nurse, in sleep profound.
The dead, the lonely dead, endure enormous pain
And when October wind strips the ageing trees,
Venting its melancholy around the marble slabs,
It dwells within the thankless still alive
Who sleep curled up warmly in their sheets
While they are eaten up alone with darkest thoughts:
Icy silent bones gnawed at by the worm
And dripped upon by soaking winter snows
As the years unfurl and no family or friend
Goes to replace the wreath that decorates the railing.

As the evening log spits and whistles in the grate
I might see her sitting calmly in her chair;
And one icy air-blue night in deep December
I might find her huddled in a corner of my room,
Solemn, having risen from her eternal bed
To cast a caring eye over her grown-up child;
What answers then could I give that pious soul
As I watch the tears drip from her hollowed empty eyes?

XVI. Brumes et Pluies

O fins d'automne, hivers, printemps trempés de boue,
Endormeuses saisons! Je vous aime et vous loue
D'envelopper ainsi mon coeur et mon cerveau
D'un linceul vaporeux et d'un vague tombeau.

Dans cette grande plaine où l'autan froid se joue,
Où par les longues nuits la girouette s'enroue,
Mon âme mieux qu'au temps du tiède renouveau
Ouvrira largement ses ailes de corbeau.

Rien n'est plus doux au coeur plein de choses funèbres,
Et sur qui dès longtemps descendent les frimas,
O blafardes saisons, reines de nos climats,

Que l'aspect permanent de vos pâles ténèbres,
—Si ce n'est, par un soir sans lune, deux à deux,
D'endormir la douleur sur un lit hasardeux.

XVI. Fog and Rain

Autumn's closure, winters and mud-bound springs
Are the passive seasons I care for and give thanks
For their encircling heart and mind
With swirling shrouds and misty tomb.

Across the wide plain where the cold wind blows
And the weather-vane rattles through the long night
My soul opens its crow's wings wider,
Far better than in the lukewarm of rebirth.

Nothing is more welcome to the cortege of my mind,
In which the hoarfrost hardened long ago,
Than the wan queen of this time
With the ashes of her universal pallor –
Unless of course, one moonless night, side by side,
We could allow our pains to sleep rocked on an uncertain bed.

XVII. Rêve Parisien

A Constantin Guys

I

De ce terrible paysage,
Tel que jamais mortel n'en vit,
Ce matin encore l'image,
Vague et lointaine, me ravit.

Le sommeil est plein de miracles!
Par un caprice singulier
J'avais banni de ces spectacles
Le végétal irrégulier,

Et, peintre fier de mon génie,
Je savourais dans mon tableau
L'enivrante monotonie
Du métal, du marbre et de l'eau.

Babel d'escaliers et d'arcades,
C'était un palais infini,
Plein de bassins et de cascades
Tombant dans l'or mat ou bruni;

Et des cataractes pesantes,
Comme des rideaux de cristal,
Se suspendaient, éblouissantes,
A des murailles de métal.

Non d'arbres, mais de colonnades
Les étangs dormants s'entouraient,
Où de gigantesques naïades,
Comme des femmes, se miraient.

Des nappes d'eau s'épanchaient, bleues,
Entre des quais roses et verts,
Pendant des millions de lieues,
Vers les confins de l'univers;

XVII. Parisian Dream

For Constantin Guys

I

A vision never seen by mortal eye
Held me trapped this morning as I woke;
A terrifying landscape, uncertain
And melting into distance.

Sleep can conjure up a world of magic!
A bizarre trick of the mind
Had removed from my vision
All traces of organic growth

And basking in the knowledge of my genius
I proudly gazed upon my picture
Held in unchanging boredom
Of water, metal, stone.

A crazy Tower of Babel made up of stairways
And arches contained a never ending palace
Of waterfalls and cascades
Tumbling into ornamental ponds;

And the weight of dense cataracts
Like the folds of crystal curtains
Hung dazzling drapes
On metal walls.

Not trees but colonnades encircled
The unmoving pools
In which gigantic naiads gazed
Like women in admiration of themselves.

Sheets of water expanded in blue
Between the quays of pink and green
Stretching out league upon league
Towards the rim of the known world;

C'étaient des pierres inouïes
Et des flots magiques; c'étaient
D'immenses glaces éblouies
Par tout ce qu'elles reflétaient!

Insouciants et taciturnes,
Des Ganges, dans le firmament,
Versaient le trésor de leurs urnes
Dans des gouffres de diament.

Architecte de mes féeries,
Je faisais, à ma volonté,
Sous un tunnel de pierreries
Passer un océan dompté;

Et tout, même la couleur noire,
Semblait fourbi, clair, irisé;
Le liquid enchâssait sa gloire
Dans le rayon cristallisé.

Nul astre d'ailleurs, nuls vestiges
De soleil, même au bas du ciel,
Pour illuminer ces prodiges,
Qui brillaient d'un feu personnel!

Et sur ces mouvantes merveilles
Planait (terrible nouveauté!
Tout pour l'oeil, rien pour les oreilles!)
Un silence d'éternité.

II

En rouvrant mes yeux pleins de flamme
J'ai vu l'horreur de mon taudis,
Et senti, rentrant dans mon âme,
La pointe des soucis maudits;

La pendule aux accents funèbres
Sonnait brutalement midi,
Et le ciel versait des ténèbres
Sur le triste monde engourdi.

Unimaginable rocks
And unprecedented waves;
Enormous mirrors cast back reflections
Of all that peered down!

Uncaring and unresponsive rivers
Like a Ganges in the sky
Poured out from urns their riches
Into diamond studded gulfs.

Designer of my own fantasy
I created out of whim
An ocean of tamed waters
Threading through a jewelled tunnel;

And all colours, even black,
Shimmered in clear light
Whilst liquid glories set
In still crystal rays.

No stars nor shafts of sunlight
Lined the sky's horizon
As this fantastic scene glowed
Entirely from within!

And over these fluid wonders
There reigned a terrifying knowledge
That all was in the eye and not the ear
As soundless eternity stretched out.

II

On opening my burning eyes
I recognised the filth of my garret room
And felt again the sharp thrust
Of cursed worries piercing
Through my soul.

With funereal repetition noon
Sounded from the clock
And the sky poured down in shadows
On the mournful numbed world.

XVIII. Le Crépuscule du Matin

La diane chantait dans les cours des casernes,
Et le vent du matin soufflait sur les lanternes.

C'était l'heure où l'essaim de rêves malfaisants
Tord sur les oreillers les bruns adolescents;
Où, comme un oeil sanglant qui palpite et qui bouge,
La lampe sur le jour fait une tache rouge;
Où l'âme, sous le poids du corps revêche et lourd,
Imite les combats de la lampe et du jour.
Comme un visage en pleurs que les brises essuient,
L'air est plein de frisson des choses qui s'enfuient,
Et l'homme est las d'écrire et la femme d'aimer.

Les maisons cà et là commençaient à fumer.
Les femmes de plaisir, la paupière livide,
Bouche ouverte, dormaient de leur sommeil stupide;
Les pauvresses, traînant leurs seins maigres et froids,
Soufflaient sur leurs tisons et soufflaient sur les doigts.
C'était l'heure où parmi le froid et la lésine
S'aggravent les douleurs des femmes en gésine;
Comme un sanglot coupé par un sang écumeux
Le chant du coq au loin déchirait l'air brumeux;
Une mer de brouillards baignait les édifices,
Et les agonisants dans le fond des hospices
Poussaient leur dernier râle en hoquets inégaux.
Les débauchés rentraient, brisés par leurs travaux.

L'aurote grelottante en robe rose et verte
S'avançait lentement sur la Seine déserte,
Et le sombre Paris, en se frottant les yeux,
Empoignait ses outils, vieillard laborieux.

XVIII. Break of Day

Reveille was sounded throughout the barracks square
And the morning breeze blew around the street-lamps.

It is the hour when a swarm of uneasy dreams
Makes restless pillow for lively adolescents;
The lamp casts a red smear like a bloodshot eye
Which throbs and pulses
Where the soul trapped in a sullen weighted body
Mirrors the conflict between lamp and day.
Like a tear-stained face which is dried in the wind
Fleeing shadows tremble in the air
Round a man who can write no more and a woman
    sated with love.

Here and there chimneys begin to smoke.
With bleary eyes and open mouth the Venus of the night
Is stunned in thick sleep.
Drooping above their scrawny freezing breasts,
Blowing on glowing embers and then on hands,
This is the hour when the cold and needy
Women in childbirth feel their sharpest pangs;
The distant cockcrow tears the foggy air apart
In a blood-choked throttled sob;
An ocean of mists rises around the buildings
And those gasping out their dying breaths in solitary wards
Release their finals gasps in heaving rattles.
The debauched return homewards worn out by their labours.

In crimson and green shivering dawn arrives
Slowly making way along the empty Seine,
As the sombre city rubs its tired eyes,
Picks up its tools: an ancient workman.

Two Rivers Press has been publishing in and about Reading
since 1994. Founded by the artist Peter Hay (1951–2003), the press
continues to delight readers, local and further afield, with its varied list
of individually designed, thought-provoking books.